OFFERING:
POETRY & PROSE BY DIANE GLANCY

Books by Diane Glancy

Offering: Poetry & Prose 1988
One Age in a Dream 1986

ᎠᎳᏂᎦᏟᏴ Offering

Poetry & Prose by
Diane Glancy

Foreword by Simon J. Ortiz

Illustrations by Terry John Swabey

Holy Cow! Press • DULUTH, MINNESOTA • 1988

ISBN 0-930100-20-4
Library of Congress Number: 86-83319

First Printing, 1988

The title, *Offering*, also appears in Cherokee.

Holy Cow! Press
P.O. Box 3170 / Mount Royal Station
Duluth, Minnesota 55803

Principal Distributor:

The Talman Company
150 Fifth Avenue
New York, New York 10011

Library of Congress Cataloging-in-Publication Data

Glancy, Diane.
    Offering : aliscolidodi.

    1. Indians of North America—Literary collections.
I. Title.
PS3557.L294034   1988   818'.5409   86-83319
ISBN 0-930100-20-4

This project is supported, in part, by a grant from the National Endowment
for the Arts in Washington, D.C., a federal agency.

TABLE OF CONTENTS

Over the past several years, mainly in literary journals and magazines, Diane Glancy has given us her vivid poetic insights into the landscape of Oklahoma and its Cherokee heritage. Now, in her *Offering,* her poetry insists more deeply and comprehensively into the dimensions of her Cherokee and German/ English birthright which, to her, is more than a matter of cultural and genetic descent. Her voice insists on "The involute Indian, the diverging white world. Parcenary: But I am not two heirs of the same inheritance, but one heir of two inheritances," urging upon us this realization. *Offering* (ALISCOLIDODI) is in a way a commemoration by Glancy of Sequoyah's achievement in transforming a foreign language into his native Cherokee. She is certain of it as she tells us "you could reach another/ from that place within a place," from ". . . a house within a house." Diane Glancy reaches toward us her offering of accomplished poetry.

—*Simon J. Ortiz*

I.

WINYAN - HCAKA

ᎠᎪᎯᏳᏍᎩ   ᏥᎩ   ᎤᏕᎩ

gohiyudisgi   tsigi   udugi

a witness   which is   hope

Her head small as a pecan.
Her body large as husks from corn.
Hi hey ya
hey yo.
She speaks in dreams.

Through narrow channels of the prairie
a stream of sheep pass into her head.
She tends them on the hill
where small rocks cluster
like a flock.

Moccasins tied to thick feet.
Her leggins dangle with puffin beaks.
She is from the north now.
Her dress fishskin.
Wooden snow goggles with slits for eyes.

Her mouth shriveled to a cedar berry
she speaks through the blue opening
in her head.
Her brittle dress crackles and her voice.
Teehee.
She laughs with narrow vision
and her small words say to me
speak.

"Bison moved through the valley at night,
their heads above the fog."

My grandmother's voice lifted the blanket it wore and
I listened to her talk.

"The mistress of the school did not like the sound of
bison,
packed cotton in her ears we saw on the table the next
morning
curled like small horns.

When she snored,
we used pieces of her cotton cloth.
No one heard anything but what came from within
where the Great Spirit called from another world.

In dreams we saw strange bison roam
and tiny sheep with cotton-wad horns.

I heard the voice of my mother once." Grandmother
went on.
"She said not to forget our ways.
She said to count my brothers.

I do not think it was her.
In the Female Seminary we learned there is no grief
in the next world
but my mother was as I remember her.
I do not think it was her.
Maybe a rabbit spoke her breath.
Maybe someone not saved by Christ.

I do not remember how many brothers I had.

But I knew the girls in camp before we scattered.
We threw game stones at rabbits
as though we were boys
and watched limbs move in ripples of the creek.

Squirrels jumped from trees.
The holy mass of clouds prowled the sky and hid in shallows
of the stream.

We chewed mullin and Jesuit's bark.
I heard a child crying once;
the voice of an older child tried to quiet it.

It was a long time ago.
I was a small girl.

Sometimes I heard a quarrel in another camp across
the hill.

I remember a hunter looking for quail
when one of our braves with an orange strip on his face
startled him.
We giggled and were punished later,
went with our fathers carrying their hatchet,
wedge, and fish gig.

We pulled off our leggings to wade in the stream.

Our brothers drew bears with arrow-marks where they wanted
their arrows to go in.

But I do not know how many brothers."

My grandmother pulled the blanket around her voice until I
lost the visions she gave me and their small, curled
voices
diminished like horns.

GREAT INDIAN FATHER IN THE SUBWAY

Father rides the subway,
mutters to himself.
The rumble of subway swims
underground,
ignites his voice.

A beaver dam under the city:
flat tail warns of low sky.
Red clouds like curved necks
of geese
weave into one hole,
out another.

Great Indian Father
sends smoke signals from
raised beaver mounds,
ancient hills where
his language rises to completion
while the subway moves
like an old man
speaking to himself.

SHORT NIGHT

I wake at four thirty when they back
the pickup to the fishing boat in the yard.
The truck dies, starts again
unfocused as the night.

Now it idles
like an old bear with an ache.
Birds start to chirp.
Somewhere in the stream
fish stir in their beds.

I try to sleep again but it fades
from my clutch.

On his birthday
an Indian gives gifts,
and I am wrapped in dark as with a shawl.

My great grandfather was born in Oklahoma,
left for the Tennessee cavalry after
an argument.
My grandmother settled in Arkansas.
My father in Missouri.

I am back in Oklahoma this early morning.
Boats rattle to the river
with bait and tackle box
while I am left squirming under the darkness
received as a gift.

Your photograph reaches me:
girl in P. S. 41, Greenwich Village School,
plaid knee-patches on your jeans,
hair parted in the middle, braided, squaw-like.

Leaves rustle in the courtyard outside the window,
children tromp the metal stairs,
walls are battered as an Indian camp.
Yet there is fire in your eyes.

It is a small memory we share.
An imperfection of thought.
One needs forgiveness to remember those years.

Grade school was the absence of anything startling,
other than the rise and fall of sun and leaves.
Thin ducks in the rain gutter.
Rotten pomegranates.
Rough wooden bowl like a trough for small hogs.

Hearing the other children in the singing room
I could not sing,
could not say anything.
I could not hit the ball across the open yard of leaves,
but waited for the passage of time.

There is no one to blame.

The teacher disliked air on her neck.
In drafts of rooms and stairs, she pulled the scarf
around her shoulders.
It was nothing, but I felt it pulled up slowly to the
jaw, over the mouth and nose.

It was only at the end of grade school
I heard her voice cling like wet leaves
and felt car tires pass on the rain-curbed street,
always the noise of traffic.

A cab bumped the school bus and we waited on the
narrow street overgrown with brownstones and
row-houses.

An old woman leaned against the black wall of the park
lost in her own world.
The teacher talked to us from hers,
counted children as we passed on the street.

Swirling leaves entered P. S. 41 from the courtyard
when we returned,
met those leaves coming out.
We hold the door politely for one another,
each speak of our own world.

Hard chairs and desks,
floors that echo the horse-tromp of children,
curdled as cucumbers and milk.

We still look for anything that will startle the eye.

War Dance At The Waldorf

The feet of Spotted Horse gallop over loose streets,
his "Hua!" hails a cab.

The driver sees us stumble into the half-night
of the city
and does not stop.

War paint on buildings,
cars with broken glass and dented fenders.
Traffic turns like the reservation windmill.
We take the subway uptown where voices sound buffalo
in prairie wind.

Spotted Horse goes into the Waldorf.
We cannot hold him back.
Red flowers bloom in the lobby above plush rugs
black as burned fields.
Peacock feathers watch us pass,
thick as brush along a country road.

Upstairs, we knock on doors.
Rooms are like the reservation:
a compartment for each one of us.
Spotted Horse stomps his feet, scares the buffalo in
his head.

"Hua!"

Men come to quiet Spotted Horse.
He thinks they are soldiers and war dances in the Waldorf
until red streets press between black curbs.

It takes a regiment to hold Spotted Horse.

We leave in a police wagon.
Spotted Horse still spouts his oracle. "Hua!"
Dust of the stampede comes from his head.

He is back on the reservation the one time the creek
rose and the cemetery fence caught brush and
twisted limbs.
Spotted Horse paddles all night in his sleep.

By morning,
we wait at the bus station in New York.
Tail of the windmill blows a crow feather,
blades turn like venetian blinds at the Waldorf.

We even go to the museum that winter
when we can get to it through the snow.
We cross Broadway at 155th,
beat our turtle-drum and deer-hoof rattle.
The pigeons aren't afraid of us;
don't fly when we pass, but stay to search-
out wild grains of grass.
We follow hawks with the snow-black shine
of feet. We are without dental records,
pork barrel, cellar.
We gather the hunger of our tribes:
Mohawk, Passamaquoddy, Penobscot, Ouray,
Chippewa, Potawatomie, Onondaga.
Rude drums, pebble-gourds,
from Long Island, Manhattan, White Plains.
We gather the basket of bones,
but even they won't burn for fire.
Parts of owls' speech hoot indifference to
spruce and pines.
We need Sacajawea to lead us like Lewis and Clark
to the other side of the continent.
It is a loud winter to travel in the northeast:
howls of the woodchuck,
his skin stretched for the drum-head; tinhorns
moving into the land.
We see with Christ-eyes the cross of trees at the
indraught of the St. Lawrence. Roar of the
bull-moose. Heye. Heye. Heye.
Our only epiphany
the scarcity of food and animal skulls with
crevices like old snow.

RESERVATION

This prairie holds us
with its plainness.
An ugly wife.
We would not stay
but children comfort us
and we need this flatness.

On our table
a carp with a tumor
on its lip,
larva eating its side.

An old man laughs,
one silver tooth
in his head
like a galvanized
watertank.

We are driven back
into the land,
our raccoon faces
banded around the eyes
with motorcycle goggles.
Every car we had
rusting in the yard.

We saddle the buffalo
and say we are captives.
This barrenness holds
us down like a wife.

PRAIRIE MASS

1.
We were ready for grace,
even before he came.
Too many years deprived of visions
we absorb the old priest who speaks
like a bleating ram,
his mouth full of baptisms and mass.
Dust from the wake of trucks our
men drive away.

His words are sudden or slow as a
herd crossing the stream.
The bells:
babies' cries we hear too often.

Reservation wind and wood ducks
cross the sky;
the sun travels north for summer.
Tribal dances jump cracks
in the floor.

The herd of our ancestors:
small now like the priest,
smaller than the altar boys who grow
as we tread creek-water.

Sun through dwarfed curtains
and new brush comb our eyes when swollen
altar boys find the road
through fields like their fathers.

Wings of ducks cup inward to the
core of ear.
The priest's words we cannot grasp.
His Christ on a stick.

2.
The world moves at a slower pace for us, lumbering under
the bitter weight of grace.

Even if we could fly with dust from the reservation road
the voice of our mothers bolts us down like ribbons.

We trim candles in the prairie church and speak our sins
in mad processions.

Father Fuego cannot understand our ways,
talks as though he were in the parish from which he came,
calls young altar boys
names of those who are gone.

3.
Trapped in buffalo thunder,
a piece of paper under bifocals
in the sun.

We ask for donors of sight.
The boys return the priest's
glasses
they hold on the steps.

The sky on fire keeps us warm.
Nights ride a patched horse:
calico quilts
old women sew
with hanging threads of mane.

We nap but cannot sleep.
North sun makes another door in
the field,
its fire burns reflected brush
in the creek
where branches
rake our bobbing heads.

Voluntary tomatoes come up in
sheep dung.
Red as the sun at dusk.

On holy days
we peel the juicy foil from the
sky,
lick the frayed hooves of horses,
lap the small red balls
for summer Christmas in our
streets.

The caw of the tiny Christ child.

LOOKING UNDER THE BED

It seems the coldest night.
Hills rise, translucent under snow as though
  the moon pulled at them like the sea.

The highway is dry   sanded during the day.
  Now traffic moves   dust to the edge of the road
making an eerie haze

                    drifting in off the ocean.
But this is prairie.
The ocean has been gone for ages.

The land is pebbled with houses and nubby farms,
                            white and uneven
as the chenille bedspread in the old house.

                You've been on the road.
Now   close enough   I can drive.

I would stay in this cold night
                but ghosts stir under the bed
    dance in a frenzy
                scalp the first white settlers
                    in the land.

Thoughts run out of my head.

    Those lonely nights   my father slept
my husband slept   children
  and I was alone and awful under the savage moon

                    wagon wheels
                caught in the slough

———————————

17

Traffic passes as usual
                          always heavy on the turnpike.

You can hear it far away at night like ocean waves.

A dirt road trails off into the distance like blades
          of a large sled.

     Red soil waits under snow.
                              Rusted radiator water.

Pines haunt these hills with spiny fossils.
Even water   frozen as it falls from
          between the rock where turnpike cuts
                                   into the hills.

This night   stirred up
                         attacking bands of Indians
     pulls me back to other nights

          moon large and white with cold.

                  ———————————

Lights from oncoming trucks
          war paint swollen on the face of the dark.

     Ghosts under my bed
walk in the hall when the floor furnace creaks at night

                    crack their knuckles
when cows fall through thin ice on farm ponds

                         pace the house
in wool masks with holes for eyes and mouths
                    striped and ghastly.

A crack in the road   wasn't there before.
     Perhaps the cold weather
                         the heavy trucks over the road

sand from the last ice storm that grinds into concrete
    like lonely nights under the single moon.

A neighbor pulled me around the block on my sled
                   when I was small

my feet   cold chunks
                    began to sting.

My brother and I jumped on the bed
   between attacks of heat from the floor furnace
        and these frigid nights

when no one passes along the turnpike without shivering.

THE WRECKER COMES

These fields seem more drab just
before the spring.
Pale branches fade into sky
and dogwoods blanch:
a dress washed too many times
stained at the hem.

My memories are white also.
You pull them from my bag
lumped as potter's clay.

We wait for the wrecker to come.
Your truck plowed too far in the ditch.
The ground is more of a feather bed
than we thought.

No wonder my ancestors feared the
pale face.
The startle of flint-lock rifle,
the bite of its fire at night.

Shooting arrows into cornstalks
I am astonished these weeds
edge their way
into plates of rocks stacked beside
the road.

You touch my leg.
Weeds tossle in the slight wind.
The truck slants sideways in the ditch.

You shape my desire with your hands
and the tires of the truck,
when pulled from the ditch,
are muddy as a potter's wheel.

TURTLES

Turtles stand on hind legs, their
spiral shells like pinwheels my father used to
nail on trees.
I hear their silent war-whoop as they spin,
hear the silent tongues of turtles,
hurp, gaw, hizz,
hind feet gnawed by animals.
Then we did not live in neighborhoods surrounded
by houses, and flying turtle-sparks
at night.
We stood on rocks like huge buffalo heads over-
looking the prairie, and turtle feet
pranced upon those heads.

TWO ANIMALS, ONE FLOOD

Day after day they caught rain in the smoke-hole
            of the teepee, sewed with curved bone
and porcupine quill, the ground limp with
                        matted grass,
stalk upon stalk like thin ancestors.
            We cup our hands with their anguished
smoke and fizzled fire. Thickets bend like ancient
                        women; barbed-wire
thickets of the white man never will have leaves,
            though they wait all summer.
                        Our tires braid the mud,
refinery smoke makes old campfires.
                        Noah's wife closes the
hole of her one-window ark. Husks of buffalo
            laugh at animals in stalls. Fires hiss
                        in the eyes of children.
Animals stand two by two, but there is only one
                        flood.

The large porcupine breathes smaller ones
        from his mouth.   They rise,
curve backward, and arch over the large one.
           They run from blazing grills of
cars and slammed surburban doors.
              Spotted hens, red deer, lope with
them on the prairie, plug-in the rain, hand-weld
                  waves to canoe.
Loose strings of light hang from antlers in the
        backyard of outerspace.
Shut out, torn away, the burning Christ still
          rises on the water.
    The porcupine speaks to himself,
             speaks hope to Christ
        from the small rainbow of porcupines.
He paddles the canoe-ark with deer and prairie hens
          over the rabbiteye and red haw.

RED STEAM

On the high plains a few
trees lean toward the north.
A ragged band of Indians.

We pick up bones from extinct animals
and old glaciers.

The sun holds a hand over our sight.
Yellow flowers, red land,
seem a vision.

The river is empty when we pass.
The water on a hunting party
will be back after rain.
The river bed, bridge, ready for its return.

Fierce wind lifts the flat sheet of fields
and the dust is red steam.

A ghostly railroad station,
disembodied.
Flying particles of soil
are bricks loosed of their burden of mortar
and sage brush caught in hedgetrees
beside the highway,
fossils of train smoke.

The Great Spirit moves across the harsh land.
Fenceposts shimmy.
A bird calling from the field just as we pass
trills in our narrow head.
We know, as we have always known,
we are not home here.

Headlights come toward us
like the white eyes of wolves,
a hungry pack
too near the barn in fog.

The morning unfolds the lick of a wolf tongue,
something out of the realm of experience,
but real, nonetheless.

A piece of spike grass pulled between the fingers.

Maybe it is the hunger of the world
that growls this foggy morning
behind the barn.

I tie up the black and white heifer,
call the chickens to the roost,
bolt the gate before the trickery of wolves
like a whip
leaves a hole in the morning
which the sun will find,
sniffing it out like the scent of blood.

TORNADO

Privets rustle
under storm winds
their white skirts tremble/

a warlord on the
prairie somewhere,
a groom, a hun, in black.

They will lose their
blossoms and bear round blue fruit.

Hail gallops
whooping rain   then silence.

Their own petals strewn before them/

the privets wait
for the choice of the warlord/

hail balls
on the ground like rice after the
abrupt nuptials.

FLOOOOOOOD

Buffalo stampede, angry the firesticks killed them.

They climb down from the death rack, return from the
spirit world with war poles.

Their fur swirls in debris. Their anger, the mud
left after water recedes.

Snowblind
in whirling storm

yellow geese with lightning-feathers
thunder-eyes

rise-fall

until yellow geese are dried-prairie-
grass-in-winter

hey na nuh
hey nuh   ho

then it made sense
when I was in the

images of that world
danced and I danced with them

knew name, face, of one another

leaves scattered holy as antelope herds
hind-feet-kicking-high

whoa bay tee
whee no   eh

THE EIGHT O FIVE

The t(rain)
again this morning, sky always gray,
grain cars f(lying)
like blackbirds with fieldseed
in their bellies.

The eight o five carrying
g(rain)
sings like tribes
when they migrated north in summer
across the plains
following tracks of herds.

High water into trees.
The lake full of rain.
We say it is someone else
pushing down on the lake
to make it spill over its edge.

While we wait
the woman earth sings with the tribes,
transforms herself
into all things.

After the train
b(rush) burning, the delay of smoke
in the car comes after
we have passed like sound.

Rain hangs fringe from earth woman's dress.
She holds the delay of truth
until it comes from our mouths.

Coyotes sleep on her lap,
birds fly into the b(ranches) of her hair
while farther down the road
the black snake train wiggles behind her ear.

INDIAN CHANT

Hunted and sung
unhunted / unsung

clump of
loghouse / chaxed hill

unuttered / unstrung

clistered bow
hunted and unsung

hunted / strung
hunted / sung.

Hunting Ground Between Word and Meaning

Bow   to arrow   (call)

take   buffalo (hide)   into your fingers
  (hear)
the feather of hawks

You   be (long)   to spirit

He   who you   are

be(cause) he   allows.

I have to look up ubiquitous again. The abstract word,
no matter how common, is hard to remember. The Indian
is rooted in the concrete. Prairie grass is everywhere.
Buffalo. The white man with his disembodied luggage
and rail-cars of reference. Visceral. Loquacious. In-
imical. Inchoate. It is like being whirled around at
the end of the line in "crack the whip". Indians must
be gullible. It is not that we cannot hold abstract
thought. To have nothing tangible is wealth. To ac-
knowledge animals without language is to bear their dig-
nity. To hear the voice of rocks. Hooves of bison.
The certainty of the deer-tail. A shadow that passes
like a chill. The strength of loaves, their "broken-
ness." Amazement that so much is made of death. A blue
sun on red fields. I am not all Indian. My great-
grandfather was the last full-blooded Cherokee relative
I have. But the intangible, Indian quality is tena-
cious as cockleburs on socks. The involute Indian, the
diverging, white world. Parcenary: But I am not two
heirs of the same inheritance, but one heir of two in-
heritances. I am sure they have a word for it.

To See Sequoyah's Cabin*

You first must enter the house built over it
then enter his:
the table, three-legged chair
and narrow ladder to loft-beds.

Perhaps it's symbolic to enter what's seen
and find a smaller duplicate inside
where he once stood with scroll and pipe
in robe and buckskin, leaning on his cane,
a turban around his head like an artichoke.

He made a Cherokee alphabet
so you could reach another
from that place within a place.

It was at that table where he sat
and pulled the prickly leaves of speech
so you could find within a sound
a language to relate, a written word that has
a meaning, a house within a house

The pungent wood-pulp smell of artichoke
fills the cedar cabin chinked with clay
where Sequoyah worked for years
making a character for each word,
but grew too many like words of someone trying
to be understood.

Then Sequoyah made a letter for each sound
he heard,
inventing characters
and using English letters, which he did not know.
He spoke only Cherokee;
spoke only from the language of the heart.

He combined the letters of the sounds
like hedge-trees gnarled with fenceposts
then stood by the table
smoking his pipe,
a written language on a scroll under his arm,
so you can work within yourself
pulling out an artichoke like a heart.

*   Sequoyah's cabin is preserved by the State Historical
    Society eleven miles northeast of Sallisaw, Oklahoma,
    on State Highway 101

SOME THOUGHTS ON OUR UNCOMMON LANGUAGE

I have trouble with the spoken word. I talk, but often
do not have the word I want to carry the meaning.
Often it is a macaronic breach of two languages—
or the snagging of one into a shortened branding-iron insignia.
Pocal is the local cowpoke.
    Chowdhurry is a quick bowl of soup.
I wonder if this happens in the transfer of two heritages
                         into one vessel—
a bifurcation of thought not only from within
but also pressed inward from the out—

I remember the neighbor woman watering her four o'clocks
in the narrow yard between our houses.

There is a word for them somewhere in my suitcase which is
packed for a long trip. You come to my house & we talk of the
flowers while the cat sprawls on the floor. I must find that
term like a dress I know is somewhere in the luggage, but with
difficulty open the grip & take out the word I need for our
conversation. Never in my mouth, falling out easily as
cornbread when I choke. No. Words are packed tightly in there.
I do not like to get them out. The isolation of the prairie has
given me a migratory sense of privacy. Words are holy as
balloons which hold our breath & that must be why it is so
hard to bear our meanings as though they were buffalo returned
    to the plains.

I remember language as a broom in the cabin / table by the
window with found objects / rocks, birdsnests, snerds, utotos,
                greesnees, snocks & eggs.

Having a child around certainly babels
the page. If I yanked the toy hammer from his hand twice,
    I've done it once.

It is now on the high shelf in the closet with the dorsal fins
if I ever return to water.

Out in back, they were building a house like Elisha & his
prophets when one chopping a tree for a beam or joist of the
house dropped it into the Jordan & said, what shall I do,
                    for it was borrowed?
And Elisha said, where is it? & he said, there.
Elisha cast a stick into the water & the axhead swam.

It is a tale we know in school:
the conjugation of the first alphabet's letter—
                    swam
                    swan
                    sway

Just then a call from the handicapped worker interrupted the
thought of the neighbor woman / the four o'clocks which opened &
closed each day at that time selling brooms & lightbulbs for a
ceiling light to see underwater & sweep the musty basement
    floor, the seeping walls.

On this trip to the mountains of Colorado where the Utes crossed
altitudes in their tract / do you know they knew when the white
        man landed?
I don't know how & they didn't know exactly who came but they
felt the intrusion of the new being.
        Epaw.   Epaw.
At one time I called grandpa chief of the beaten tribe who
wandered with moccasins on the wrong feet.

Some new object which would have to be named in the genre of
neu-essayist when there is no nouveau object to name but there
it was they knew somehow.

Diurnal. The name of the flower & the daily opening & closing
between the herds of stars grazing black, transparent fields.

Not the sweet neighbor watering her diurnals but something that
would plant this square cement box in the ground & call it
basement.

Oh, they are only places to wash the clothes. Wringer & the
lines of rope across the basement ceiling under the joists for
the living room floor upstairs.

Once in church camp in Colorado we didn't want to drive
the 400 miles across Kansas in the heat
& took Trail Ridge over the mountains down through Berthoud
Pass / Battered by the time dark
passed over us in Kansas. El Jebel. Tabernash. Sawput.
                    I said the names we passed.

My ancestors returned from the sweat lodge
                    ebbulant as tall grass
mule-lol-ling the prairie
coming to grips with new words
nue udderings sometimes not words
but sound oozing like grease from under the axel rods.
                    Words are the building blocks,
the diurnals that blooM each day,
make the garden in which we Roamp.   Roam or Romp.   Possibly
                    Rump.

We unravel the navel & pour out ourselves
like Christ on the cross
when they pierced his side or when I pull the plug
in the sink after I finish washing underwear
                    to hear the loud suck.
And hang it over the pole & it splats in the tub just like
afternoon rain in the mountains at church camp when I
felt the spirit falling & didn't know the word to say but said
                    Ey co bah/ eet/ eet/
                    Somehow they knew.

The balloon's navel all puckered where we put in our breath.
That's what our words do—
                    Highjack four o'clocks.

Upsidedown on the floor—   her hind legs spread—
the cat is my daughter when she was a baby in leggins or
                    leotards swollen with diaper.
Now the cat is a baby I hold.

At one time our words were kiva,
            grandpa chief
        storing the broken parts of our tribe.

III.

START OF A LONG TRIP

The sun comes up like a ceiling light in my eyes.
It was dark when we drove toward the mountains
and through them.
Now in the east,
the sun is vivid as nightmares.
Long shadows, black as light cords, plug into bushes.
Piñons glimmer with dew and we praise the dawn
when all things seem connected.

SOLAR ECLIPSE, MAY 30, 1984

Each morning
I wake invisible.

I make a needle
from a porcupine quill,
sew feet to legs,
lift spine onto my thighs.

I put on my rib and collarbone.

I pin an ear to my head,
hear the waxwing's yellow cry.
I open my mouth for purple berries,
stick on periwinkle eyes.

I almost know what it is to be seen.

My throat enlarges from anger.
I make a hand to hold my pain.

My heart a hole the size of the sun's eclipse.
I push through the dark circle's
tattered edge of light.

All day I struggle with one hair after another
until the moon moves from the face of the sun
and there is a strange light
as though from a kerosene lamp in a cabin.

I put on a dress,
a shawl over my shoulders.

My threads knotted and scissors gleaming.

Now I know I am seen.
I have a shadow.
I extend my arms,
dance and chant in the sun's new light.

I put a hat and coat on my shadow,
another larger dress.
I put on more shawls and blouses and underskirts
until even the shadow has substance.

DEER WOMAN

All afternoon.
we drive and don't get anywhere.
The pale moon a teepee smoke-hole.
Drawings circle the hide.
Sleep waits for us by the road
and eyes shut
without return to the land.
The straight stems of berries
hold stubbornly to the bush.
We swim the evening,
would float through the smoke-hole,
but now the moon is hard.
Maybe we are in Deer Woman's trap.
Surely the last of the clouds
are like the white buckskin she wears.
We look under the hem for hooves.
The sky is heavy.
The moon a plug we must pull.
Then Deer Woman has us in her mouth.
She shakes until we are senseless
as our sleep.
We beg to go back and leave a warning:
Deer Woman waits
behind the popping moon.

The wind lfts   her fte
stomp-
          dances in the leaves

She is n/even quiet
before the ceremonial fire

We are ashamed of her
     buckskin above her knees

Hi yey ki ay
she shimmeys in the dust on sacred ground

Our skirts are full as brussel sprouts
          wool scarves around our heads
a pail of beets in our hands

we hold the vision of flames
to the dark blood-
shed of our race
               ig-
noring the geese
the hus-
tle bump of the wind

She enrages the fire until antlers lift from the blaze
a mad buck pawing the ground

The wind will not be quiet but minces in the dust
her opossujm belly
red jelly eyes

She kicks on these loud nights
attacks the sky w/clouds
          where she will n/ let us pass

THE SPIRIT BLESSES YOU W/HARDSHIP

Your horse and buffalo are gone. Your squaw and gun.
Lights in prairie towns are stars you follow. If
scattered tribes were brought together, their brilliance
would startle you. But you are not bound to this world.
You migrate to the next. Cattle in feedlots. You feel
the prod. The dark soil of a prairie hill is the ramp
you walk/pushed into the open mouth of the twinkling
universe.

KIOWA DANCERS

After shinny games
>> and the woman's round dance

lodge singers chant
>> Hi yay hay yay
>>> hi yay hay yee.

After winter count
and the issue of rations from Fort Sill

Chester Left Hand   Mopope   Poolaw
>> ghost dance.

They dance until wild game & ancestors return.

They dance frantic
>> in prairie wind:
beef rations drying on the line.

SEEKING THE IROQUOIS THAT INHABITED PENNSYLVANIA
CARNEGIE MUSEUM OF NATURAL HISTORY, PITTSBURGH

On the last floor   in back

a few glass cases
like a primer for the dull

    dancing stick
    smoking pipe
    throwing ax

Indians almost real spin and weave

    kwasha   dress
    haka napha   leggins
    kwawa   belt

but Hopi, Zuni, Papago,
as though there were no tribes from the northeast.

But down the hall
a collection of dragonflies in another room.

I leave a sign: old biplanes

on a mission of search and find.

Don't fiddle with that, said Hustwayte's wife.
The sash was from the Indian girl, who used to
stand in the shade of the cabin before it was
house, when it was a half-faced camp: a cabin
with three walls. The girl waited for the
cracker Hustwayte's wife gave her. She licked
salt from it until it was soggy as a shriveled
piece of moon. Hustwayte's wife wouldn't let
me near her. The Indian girl might have lice.
She gave the girl two thimbles which she put
on the sash, not knowing what else to do with
them, tinkling faint laughter as she walked.
Leaning back in the chair against the open door,
killed buffalo herds for hides and tongues.
The Indian girl's shadow at the cabin like a
dank buffalo rotting in the sun. Sinews for
strings of bows. Harsh as prairie she waited,
said nothing most of the time, reached for
crackers ee yatos mago. Soldier's bowlegs from
saddles and arrows of hunger. Montana, Kansas,
Dakota like deer horns on the mantel. The
wife's glasses paned windows uneven as horses
lying down the first time she could see her
shadow. Crackers awkward as reclining horses
seventy ghosts in the hills. Harsh as prairie
e aa bag sagus called fiddle laughter.

REQUIEM FOR A CHILD

> He an na, hah.
> Ya ho o ay.
> Hey ho ye nay.

We miss you, He an na,
black hair straight as cemetery pines,
face flushed as rhubarb.

We wipe the sprinkles
from your lips,
wrap you in a shawl.

Now you sleep in the earth
guarded by a grotesque bear.

In that place you hurt
wings will sprout like stalks
and you will fly.

We remember you, child,
drenched in rain
as we stand severed from the cold sky.

BLIND INDIAN

His flame   mouth
speaks visions
        rusts the roof

In winter   fuchsia snows
        fall

a green dormer
ruffled peak

where chimney smoke rises

        a dark rose.

INDIAN GIRL BORED WITH CEREMONIES

She reads in the sun,
knees drawn up to her chest
while men play stick ball,
hitting the wood fish on a pole
with a small rock.

An unseen stream moves before her eyes
as though she watches fish.

Peace pipe,
prayers and dance.

The moon rises on its pole.
                              Way ha nay.

She closes her book.

In the medicine fire,
cracked bark of burning logs.
Sparks coil fish on sacred ground.
Heat runs like rabbits.

The words that entered her head still
swim before her eyes when she sleeps.

All night she dreams
until she wakes
clutching a small rock in her hand.

Death does not come easy to an iron horse.
No shot is fired, no wolves fight for the carcass.
The old train is left to rust for years.
Dampness rises on mornings after snow
and makes ghostly passengers detained from
passing through Indian lands.
Old routes eventually had military protection
from Bismark to the Black Hills to Wyoming.
Shoshone, Blackfoot, Flathead.
Such names were in the mouths of boys.
Their mothers shuddered to hear of them
and told them to be quiet.
The war-path of the train took northern passes
through the pines, followed galloping telegraph-
wires between black poles.
In Helter, Red Rock, Dry Gulch,
dogs barked silently in the noise of arrival.
Death is never easy.
No weeping funeral guests, no geysers mark the grave;
only northern plains, the rotting hulk of
train, and ghostly passengers hovering near their
baptism in steam.
They pull their coats around them,
would rise, but cannot get away.
In the pines, the white moon has the eye
of an owl before it fades into day like an onion.
The cold wind makes them cry.
A screech owl echoes the metal whinny of the
iron horse and train-smoke held by gravity
crawls along the ground.
Soldiers, women and boys, wait among the
trunks and satchels on the station platform;
the iron horse disintegrates under northern
prairie snows.
No men come searching for them like those who looked
for Elijah when he was gone.
Or they wait for Elijah himself to come back,

stretch himself upon them, and sneeze seven times,
so they can get up and dance in the pines.

We feel them for some time now,
a residue as though from a dream,
watching from the crawling hills
and lines of trees in the draw:
Chief Black Kettle and his tribe,
frozen white as clouds in the sun.

Gullies gouge the red soil like war-
paint but there was not time for that
when Custer waited the night in a
blizzard and rode at dawn from the
ridge into the Cheyenne winter camp.

In the museum: stirrup, bit, rifle-
shells, pouch, arrowheads from the
battle ground; and from the hills,
a pack-mule feed-bag and a soldier's
mess kettle, dented as old maps
of attack plans.

Like dreams, it all takes place
in an instant. From the moment
I hear the sound until I wake,
you say is only seconds. Between
the cats fighting outside the
window this morning is my long dream.

And here, in glass cases, relics of
the Seventh Cavalry and a tribe
of Indians. A chief who wanted peace.
A general who fought for westward
expansion.

Down the road, under a circular
break in the clouds, an irrigation-
pipe on crude tractor-wheels
washes their battlefield.

An early morning dream returns:
a werewolf with black hair on its face,
tied up, held captive with others
in beds. I walk past them
and someone sprays vinegar-water.
I brush it away with irritation,
and the snarling cats wake me.
I cannot sleep again to find what happens.

Black Kettle had his own dream of a
wolf with blood on its face and knew
they would die, like all of us,
but not when.

Now I stand on the road where Custer
waited. Some of the artifacts
from two races still buried in the ground.
A strange time warp hidden
like the end of a dream.

I look at the Washita Creek where
Black Kettle fell, and his wife with him,
a few yards away. The tribe still
running in all ways.

Before they could bury him, his flesh
was torn by wolves
as though he once dreamed he would die,
knowing at last, it would be then.

In the draw, the Indian tribe thaws.
They speak with sign language like trees.
The sudden smell of wet buffalo robes,
and a small howl from the soft lining
of the throat.

We listen to winds over the grasslands:
once through this country is enough.

RESERVATION SCHOOL FOR GIRLS

I.
We hang clothes on the line.
His wide trousers and shirt, wind-beat,
roar small thunder from one prairie cloud.

The same rapple of flag on its pole.

Half in fear, half in jest, we laugh.
He calls us crow women.
Our black hair shines in the sun
and in the light from school windows.

He drives his car to town, upsets the dust
on buckboard hills.
We sit on the fence when he is gone.
Does he know we speak of thunder in his shirts?

We cannot do well in his school.
He reads from west to east.
The sun we follow moves the other way.

Crowbar.

Our eyes come loose from words on the page
in narrow rooms of the reservation school.
He perceives and deciphers at once.

For us
written letters will not stay on the page,
but fall like crows from the sky and hit
against the glass windows of the school.

Our day is night when we sit in rows of the classroom.
Leaves in a whirlwind from sumac groves.
Flock of crows are black stars on a white night.

II.
On the porch of the reservation school
the backbirds walk around our feet,
fly into our head.
They call our secret name.

Dark corridors linger in our mind
We whisper the plains to one another.

We do not talk of what we cannot understand.
Black and white fleckered dresses.

Our face like our fathers.

The sun is no enemy to the eye looking west.
The brush thin as hair of old ones.

It blinds the eye, makes fire on fields,
flashes against windows like silver ribbons
on burial robes.

Hot late into the fall, windy, ready for
cold to sweep in.
The heat seems solid, but totters on the brink
of winter.

We laugh to ourselves when he returns to the
reservation school for girls.
Take his clothes from the line.
Set the table with salt and pepper, spoon, knives.
Cattails and milk-pods in a jar.

We get lard from the basement,
rub a place in the dusty window like a moon in the
ancient sky.

III.
One hill larger than the others:
an old buffalo with heavy head and whiskers
nods at the ground,
grazes on my dreams, one blade at a time.

We stay in our stiff white-sheeted beds in the
dormitory room.
Buffalo wander in our dreams.

White night-dresses.
Black pods suspended in sumac groves like crows.

In the sweat lodge of sleep
we make our vision quest,
black as pitch in crevice between crow feathers.

We hang his thunder clothes in sleep,
arms reach above our beds like willows blowing slowly
by the creek.

Quietly we choke,
hold our wounded arms like papooses.

Clothes beat on lines.
Sumac groves and whirl of leaves:
a shadow of our fathers at council fires.

Red leaves, waxy as hay on fields.
We dream of schoolrooms.

Written letters on the wind.

He reads crow-marks on the page but does not know
crow.

Photo Frames #1-11, Kansas City Stockyards

(Or How To Be Indian)

The world we seek is white.
Barret Watten
Note

. . . language is a surprising tool,
recently I turned around and was
kind of astonished what can be
done with it.
Larry Eigner
Approaching things Some Calculus
Of Everyday Life
How figure it   Experience

Father, you are the absolute I struggle toward all my life, and the absolute I struggle away from. Maybe it is so for only daughters who are first born and physically like the father, a similarity neither of us want yet are proud of somehow.

At sixty miles an hour, after your funeral, it seems I hardly move. A few angus blow past like cardboard boxes in the wind. An old house leans into the prairie like your head against the back of the chair all those afternoons you dozed. A feeling knocks about in the head like wrapping papers in the garage when you forgot to put down the door, and the wind or a neighbor's dog sniffed them out.

We moved more times than I can remember. Always on the road you knew the names of ducks and clouds. You knew the name of evening. I saw only the highway into the narrow universe and knew when your heart began to slow like a large clock in an old farmhouse.

It seems we always moved and didn't get anywhere. Hey yey yee. Indian chants oozed from your heritage in those dreams everyone has: we run in place as though treading air and never escape what pursued us.

FRAME #1

Father, you were leader of the animals in the stockyards, finally plant superintendent. I loved you, hated you, father, I carry your anger like cattle prod. What is it we could never settle? A pin-hole camera I look into and find only parts of what must be whole.

You came to the stockyards in Kansas City before I was born, lived there until I was eleven. You were transferred again and again. We moved but always traveled back to Kansas City to see the family.

When we were still in Kansas City I went to work with you on Saturdays. We turned left onto the Twelfth Street Viaduct and drove down the upper level, making a journey from Kansas City, Missouri, on the bluffs, to Kansas City, Kansas, in the riverbottoms.

Our blue 39 Dodge seemed a spirit vision. I stood close to you when I was small. Later I sat on my side of the car with an arm resting on the window. From the stockyards we returned on the lower level of the viaduct because I asked you to.

In the summer of 1951, the Kaw River flooded, passing over the stockyards and nearly climbing the Twelfth Street Viaduct with its cargo of dead pigs. The water almost followed the tenuous road on the side of the bluff into the Argentine district of Kansas City where the progeny of early cattle drovers from New Mexico live.

FRAME #2

It was after the flood you were transferred to packing houses in several midwestern towns. On our trips back to Kansas City, we always drove to the stockyards to see Armour's, returning on the eerie lower level of the viaduct, where shafts of sunlight pinholed the vast arches, flickering when we passed, as though we were on a triumphant return from the hunt.

In 1968, Armour's in Kansas City was razed. Hogs and cattle would be killed and processed in the same place they were born, eliminating their long and expensive transport by truck or rail. It was our last trip together down the glorious conduit that carried traffic into the stockyards, spilling its sense of history into the forum of the Livestock Exchange, the coliseum of cattle pens, and the sulphur baths of the West End Hotel.

Father, you are dead now also, and the stockyards with you, and yet you are alive. I am still the quantum of small papoose who would hunt your world.

FRAME #3

In the old days, there were 4,200 cattle pens, 700 hog pens, 400 sheep pens and 15 brick mule and horse barns. I have a yellowed newspaper clipping. The record was set on October 19, 1943, when 64,015 cattle were yarded. You were there that day, father, and all those days the stockyards thrived in its glory, and when it dried up, you shriveled with it. The final sleep toward which you always leaned from your chair in the living room.

FRAME #4

Father, after your funeral, there is still a cattle pen of language between us, the chute directly to the kill, old lead bull, I follow you up the ramp and you step aside and leave me to face the sudden end before I am ready to leave you and be strung upsidedown blood spilling to the slaughtering floor.

I look at you with the pink eye that swept the cattle yards. The bags of bone fertilizer. Leaves should be white also we should be at peace but I am drowsy as you.

Clouds pass in the high sky like Indians on the ghost trail you now follow on this long journey is to be Indian, having no place to go but going anyway. The moving grasses remind me of our trail. You, father, brought me here, to this chair where I sit after your funeral. Hee too bay. Waves of the sea slant away from Kansas City back into our ancient wandering before our way of life was pulled off us like skin from cows.

The barren moon on the cattle yard.

Now you have the sleep you lost.

Moo.

FRAME #5

In the kitchen a pomegranate & pepper Halved. I rinse the lungs of the pepper in cold water.

flat seeds

tiny white bats

clustered in their caves

cut across with a knife slit in the neck

These tiny seeds like so many pots & pans Hanging over us in the roof of the kitchen

the attic above which we move like the dreams of cows after their death

In you, father, some chambered part cut into my heart, dug out these small clustered moons.

a tribe no longer on its land
even coyotes laugh
Anger oozes OOZES

when the wind is out of the west the smell of cattle yards climbs the bluff and raids Kansas City the nice buildings behaving themselves and clustered like my heart. I take my paring knife or spoon gut them myself yes I would. To be Indian is to have the heart of revenge and to not know where to unload nor how is hidden the old way of life that howls in the night the coyotes they beat off of holding pens before the cattle were loaded into railroad cars and taken to Kansas City.

FRAME #6

In this picture
(which comes from our images upsidedown in the camera
like cattle Hanging in lockers
stripped of hooves, tails, heads
after the kill)

we are standing by one another the Fence in the background a line cut into the horizon or a line of thought from your head which you never shared with me and yet it bound everything I knew

Maybe the anger stems from that and grows up like devil's claw that catches around the cattle's hooves

Oh This is where I am much older see I am tall as you with my son when he was a baby and I visited you and wanted to drive the car to Kansas City when you lived not fifty miles and you wouldn't let me have your car and I felt backed again into a corner Helpless because you had the car and money and I had none and asked you for them but you held power over me and I was MAD yelled at you screamed I would do what I want LEFT the next day and would not be your INDIAN because

how to be an Indian is not to be

and how I LONGED for my own existence independent of you who had my feet I needed for the bottom of my legs so I could walk. You make it hard for me this noise between us that is only moos and how can I be free of you now that I am gone from you? You are the other side of the enclosure with all the names you knew and we are not together why would I want to be?

67

FRAME #7

In
jun
air
rows
(inbreath)
ssstthhhuuuuuuuuuummmmmmmpp!
less
un
us
from
strife
cat
tul
tipped
eee
broke
um
wur
dses
Hey yey hee yee
the farthur
father
you are
than before
I track
your trail of
cat
tul

FRAME #8

Now back down the road we travel all the way to the old place the dirt road the drive into the yard the porch the large tree Father we are Home all the moons we had clustered in this pepper I cut into after your funeral
You were never clearer than on this day under the air cold as a glass window the shade of the winter tree a net fallen over us
consumed like steaks and ribs you brought from the stockyards.

FRAME #9

I know the highway through this land
spirit road
just where it passes
I feel the movement of traffic all things slow and fast caught in their own pace their own realm passing through one another
simultaneously
the war you don't want me to see when I travel with you all the time this tortured life of neglect and want finally makes inroads and I feel what you feel father
small intervals of the album on my lap
I am angry you never shared it with me I am angry over your anger that sometimes oozed out of you like a bull that tried to climb the fence the times you whipped me as though I were a scared cow that didn't know where the gate was to the loading car
(which was and is and will be)

FRAME #10

Father you should have known I would return the small, dark child you loved.

FRAME #11

and it is all right because it will be where there is a place we are herded and our snot is wiped our bruised and bruising hooves are healed our diseases washed and we are
CLEAN

and whole and it is the place we should dream of in our spirit dreams the marks we should draw on our teepees and walls of our house but try to be ready in it while you are a body on four legs a mouth that opens and moos with slobbers

we should forget our bad times relish the good with delight like pomegranates bursting from their seeds and have it here in our album so it is a pinhole back into the life we had and one interval will not have to jump another the way a train track used to take cattle to the yards and we would drive down the viaduct in Kansas City where you will be again father

when I arrive
your face smiling
your arms open wide.

Acknowledgement to *Napa Review* for "Great Great Grandmother Steps into the Room"; *Calyx* for "Lunar Eclipse," "Great Indian Father in the Subway," and "Snowblind"; *Songs from This Earth on Turtle's Back* (Greenfield Review) for "Two Animals, One Flood" and "There Won't Be Another"; *Nimrod* for "Museum of the American Indian, New York"; *These Hearts, These Poems: An Anthology of New American Indian Poetry* (Pueblo of Acoma Press) for "Female Seminary, Tahlequah, Indian Territory," "Red Steam," and "To See Sequoyah's Cabin"; *Black River Poets* for "Fog"; *The Clouds Threw This Light* (Institute of American Indian Arts Press, Santa Fe) for "Reservation School for Girls"; *South Florida Poetry Review* for "Turtles"; *Maelstrom Press* for "Reservation" and "Requiem for a Child"; *Crosscurrents* for "Eight O Five"; *Fiddlehead* for "The Wrecker Comes"; *Encore* (Albuquerque) for "Black Kettle Grasslands, Western Oklahoma"; *HOW(ever)* for "Hunting Ground Between Word and Meaning," "Indian Chant," and "Blind Indian"; *Paragraphs* for "Hustwayte's Wife"; *Native Arts Update* for "Kiowa Dancers" and "Seeking the Iroquois"; *Sulphur* for "Some Thoughts on Our Uncommon Language"; *Wicazo Sa Review* for "Photo Frames #1-11, Kansas City Stockyards (Or How to be Indian)," *Akwekon Literary Review* for "Female Seminary, Tahlequah, Indian Territory"; *Sphinx, Women's International Literary Review* for "Reservation School for Girls"; *Prickly Pear Poetry Journal* for "Short Night"; *Syncopation* for "Solar Eclipse, May 30, 1984."

Diane Glancy was born in Kansas City, Missouri, in 1941, of a German/English mother and a Cherokee father. She was educated at the University of Missouri and received her M.A. from Central State University in Oklahoma. She has lived in Tulsa where she was Artist-in-Residence for the State Arts Council. Her poems and stories are widely published in such journals as *The Kansas Quarterly, Ploughshares, Cutbank, Ironwood, New Letters, Sulfur, Prairie Schooner, Hiram Poetry Review, The Mississippi Review, North Dakota Quarterly, Awkesasne, Nimrod, Cincinnati Poetry Review* and *Helicon Nine*. Her chapbook of poems, *Brown Wolf Leaves the Res*, was published in 1984 by Blue Cloud Quarterly and won the Pegasus Award from The Oklahoma Federation of Writers. A full-length collection of poems, *One Age in a Dream*, won the Lakes and Prairies Prize from Milkweed Chronicle and was published in the fall of 1986. She is one of 12 writers in a volume of Indian biographies, *I Tell You Now*, published in 1987 by the University of Nebraska Press and The Cooper Union. Ms. Glancy also won the Five Civilized Tribes playwriting contest and was the 1984-86 Laureate. She has two children who attend Oklahoma State University and The University of Kansas. In 1988 Ms. Glancy received her M.F.A. from The University of Iowa and she currently teaches at Macalester College in Saint Paul, Minnesota.

41 . 51